FELINE ASTROLOGY:

The Horoscope,
for Your Cat,
You Never Knew You
Needed

Clair Lofthouse

For my cats, River and Trickle.

Obviously.

Table of Contents

"Beauty begins
the moment you
decide to get a
cat"

- Some Fashionable Cat

Astrology for Cats?

Say what you will about astrology, but it has been used for thousands of years by humans who wanted to understand other humans and their own humanness.

To think that only ONE species on Earth is affected by the planets and stars in the sky at the time of birth would be ridiculous.

This book gives you a fighting chance of understanding the basics of your cat's psyche. But just like knowing a human's Sun Sign will not bring to light every facet of their complex personality, values, and beliefs, knowing your cat's Sun Sign will not either. They are even more complex than humans... really!

Sun Signs are just the tip of the cosmic iceberg known as astrology. There are also Moon Signs and Rising Signs that add depth to the individual cat. This is what sets one Taurus cat apart from the other—they were born at different times of the day. So it is really unlikely for two cats to have the exact same Sun, Moon and Rising signs and therefore, they are different cats.

But let's be real...

It is hoped you rescued your cat. Which means you probably do not know what day Charles Digby

Wigglesworth III (or CD-Dubbs3 as his friends call him) was born, let alone the time. Perhaps you have a close enough guesstimate to at least narrow down the Sun Sign but you may be flying blind.

So read the following pages closely. If your rescue cat came with an estimated birthday of April 10 but seems more Taurus than Aries, then maybe his birthday is wrong.

But what if your cat was born in your garage and you are one hundred percent sure that CD-Dubbs3 came out third, right after Pussington and before Muffins Galore at 12:36pm, April 10 and the dude is not fiery like an Aries should be? There is this thing called life experience and choice—your cat has had the first and used the second.

Astrology is like an exercise for our brain to tune in to the intricacies of the personalities around us. It can bring awareness to ideas and ways of thinking that we may never have thought other people subscribe to before, but it is not an operation manual.

As for cats, they definitely think differently than us. So, here is the horoscope you never knew you needed for your cat because when it comes to understanding our cats, we need all the help we can get.

All the Signs: Sun, Moon and Rising

You know Charles Digby Wigglesworth III as well as anyone because you share his home. So you see the Sun Sign—his basic outward characteristics.

The Moon Sign is all about the internal life of each cat. These are the instinctual patterns of your cat, the parts of him that are suppressed by clockwork meal times, vet visits, and (mostly consensual) petting.

However, there is a third layer. Invite someone into your home (we will maintain the facade of you having any ownership of things that actually belong to your cat) and they will have a different impression of your cat than you do. This impression is explained by the Rising Sign.

Think of it this way...

The Sun Sign reflects how you see your cat.
The Moon Sign reflects how your cat sees himself.
The Rising Sign is how most people see your cat.

If the Sun Sign does not fully explain your cat, understand that it is an incomplete picture. If you manage to figure out the Rising Sign and Moon Sign for your cat, read the horoscope for those signs too in order to gain a better understanding of your cat.

This book also addresses cusps of each sign. If a cat is born in the very end of one sign or at the start of another, their personality may reflect a blend of the signs they are between. Again, this is tricky for rescued animals where a birthdate may be their "Gotcha Day" or an estimate based on teeth health. Use your discretion as you learn more about your cat to figure out which sign they are. Astrology is most powerful when used as a flashlight to illuminate and bring consciousness and awareness of what is already known.

How This Works

The following pages break down each of the twelve horoscope signs and give you real, applicable, useful information that will help you improve relations with your cat. Even if everything is fine, there is always room to improve.

In the interest of fairness, each chapter alternates between male and female pronouns when referring to cats.

This book features a broad range of cats, fosters and rescues in the hopes of inspiring the reader. Every cat featured in this book has been rescued or has something adorably different about them. What makes these cats different is also what gives them power and renders them special, unique and worthy. The author's cats also feature heavily throughout. River is the tabby and Trickle, the Lynx Point. Both are rescues.

"Be the cat you want to see in the world"

- Some Humanitarian Cat

ARIES

March 21st - April 15th

DUALITY: Masculine

ELEMENT: Fire

QUALITY: Cardinal

PERFECT COLLAR COLOR: Red

FAVORITE TOY: Wand toy ("Flies like a real bird!")

WEAKNESS: Not so good at sticking the landing

It is not your house. It is your cat's house. You just live in it.

You are lucky enough to be employed (for no pay, frequent scratches and only so long as you dispense a daily supply of treats) by the best boss in the world—your Aries cat.

Aries cats pull all the strings. They have got you trained; you follow their schedule and you like it. Your needs come second to those of your Aries feline.

That said, you would miss the little girlie if she was not around. What purpose would your life have?

Your Aries cat is assertive, fiery, energetic, independent, bold and sometimes aggressive (but super cute). Your cat will accept you if she knows that the relationship benefits her.

Aries was the god of war, so expect not just a tendency towards taking action, but tactics, strategy and the ruthlessness of a being that knows not what failure means. She has got major Sun Tzu, Wolf of Wall Street, Shark Tank vibes.

Thanks to their energy and boldness, these cats play hard. It is recommended you find a wand toy that your cat likes and bond with your cat through play, because they are not going to find contentment from sitting on your lap alone. Wand toys are perfect because they give your cat the challenge she craves. They move fast and unpredictably, giving your cat the chance to break out the skills that often lay dormant in her sheltered life. Even though everyone knows that cats are the world's most effective killers, she still wants to prove it.

While offering a challenge, it also keeps you out of the arena and in the game master position instead. Some say humans are superior, but we are mere mortals and the dozen tiny razor blades attached to Mrs. Fluffins will be your undoing!

Any games that keep your fiery cat away from

This adorable kitten is named Aries, so of course she is our model for her namesake. Aries once spent her days by the trash cans, and nights huddled in the basement of a nearby building she was not officially allowed to be in. Now she spends her nights sleeping under the covers thanks to Little Wanderers!

Little Wanderers is an all volunteer 501(c)(3) charity that focuses on rescue and Trap—Neuter—Return (TNR) program of stray and feral cats in some of the toughest neighborhoods in New York City. Little Wanderers fully vetted Aries, found her a foster home and then found her an amazing adopter.

your fragile human body will be best. Your cat will appreciate the space and will love you even more for respecting their independence. You will also save on bandaids!

These cats lose interest in toys very quickly. New is always better, so make sure to have a few toys in rotation so a fresh toy can appear just before Pussington loses interest.

Aries cats may sound like jerks, and they can be,

but they are not all bad. As the first sign of the zodiac, they are the baby—they want to be loved and coddled. They are optimistic, naive and quirky. Trickle is an Aries!

Cusps of Aries

March 21 - March 25
Aries with Pisces tendencies. Your cat is a precious snowflake; she is unique and special. She is a little fiery, but loving and sweet. Impulsive and smart, but able to go with the flow, too. She will be creative with her toys and can play with a pen or Q-tip for hours.

April 15 - April 19
Aries with Taurus tendencies. Energy... Lots of it. Emotions rule your cat's life. Feeling out of control or surrounded by mess makes these cats irritable. Joy and excitement are just as strong as despondency for these cats. Whatever they do, they do fully.

TAURUS
April 20th - May 20th

DUALITY: Feminine

ELEMENT: Earth

QUALITY: Fixed

PERFECT COLLAR COLOR: Pale blue

FAVORITE TOY: Cardboard scratcher
on the ground

WEAKNESS: Freaking out in the car

Couch potato. Foodie. Spoiled. Bed hog.

If you have called your cat any of these things, then he is probably a Taurus. These cats are all about comfort and the best things in life. They want the richest canned foods, the fluffiest toys and the comfiest cat beds—although you are more likely to find your cat taking up the majority of your own bed.

Taurus cats love to be petted and held, and they will ask for it—but only for a nanosecond, because he is a cat, after all. This is not news!

Taurus is ruled by Venus, the planet of all things beautiful. Venus is also the planet of love, so be ready for many displays of affection from your cat.

However, Taurus cats are also known for their determination, stubbornness, and dislike of change. They like what they like, so do not expect them to change their favorite nap spot on a whim.

They will be consistent about their preferred food type; if you have to switch it up, do so incrementally. For the first couple of days have a ¼ serving of new food to a ¾ serving of old food. After those first couple of days, transition to ½ new and ½ old. Two more days pass until you transition to ¾ new food and ¼ old food. Finally, after at least six days of transition, serve one hundred percent new food, providing your cat has touched that food this whole time. If they have not been eating the new food, you should stop this process; it is very important that cats do not skip meals, as their metabolism makes eating frequently a necessity. For more information, contact your veterinarian.

Perhaps Taurus cats love their food so much because it is comforting, and Taurus cats love their creature comforts. You may want to listen to your veterinarian if he or she says that your cat is on the heavier side. Use portion control tactics with your cat, instead of free feeding as much as he will eat.

They love anything that makes them feel cozy and loved, so you may be required to pet them for the duration of your time together sitting on the couch watching TV.

Since these cats hiss at change, vet visits are nearly impossible.

If your Taurus cat vanishes into thin air when the cat carrier comes out, try appealing to the Taurus' need for consistency by keeping it out around the house all the time. This way, the carrier becomes part of home and the status quo—both things that Taurus cats love. Putting some of the finest cat treats in it will also appeal to the Taurus love of yummy food.

If after a few months, your overly cautious cat still refuses to go near the carrier, you can always find a mobile vet to come to your home-loving, change-averse little bull-cat!

"When words fail,
meows speak"

- Some Elizabethan Cat

@sister.tippy.cat

It is often our struggles that connect us with others, human and feline, alike. Tippy's story is an example of a bond formed over shared experience. Tippy had experienced chronic ear infections since she was born, and her previous owner had tried to remedy her earaches by putting hydrogen peroxide into her ear not realizing that she was doing more harm than good. Tippy's ear problems worsened until she went into rescue, where Deanna became her foster mom. Tippy's head was clearly already tipping. What started as a foster became a forever home. This close friendship was in part because Deanna had true empathy for Tippy's condition—Deanna had sustained a traumatic brain injury in an accident years earlier. She had undergone her own surgeries and still experiences episodes of vertigo, just like Tippy. Despite her condition, Tippy is happy and active, tilt and all! She enjoys bird watching and loves treats. Her cute little head, positioned to the left leaves her appearing to be inquisitive to every sound and activity. #livinglifetippy

Before entering rescue and finding her way to Deanna of @sister.tippy.cat, Gretta was known as "Grunty Runty". The family that gave her that name had approached a veterinarian to put Gretta to sleep because she "wasn't good enough" (we strongly disagree). Gretta was born without a right eye and with a jaw malocclusion, thus giving her a shifted jaw and a cute little snaggletooth! The veterinarian refused to do the euthanasia and instead "Grunty Runty" went into rescue. With a new name and lease on life, Gretta started gaining confidence and trust in humans again in her forever home with Deanna. Nowadays, she lives for soft push up treats, laying on laps, and more treats! #Grettathegremlin

Cusps of Taurus

April 20 - April 24
Taurus with Aries tendencies. These cats are self-sufficient and independent. However, they are great companions when you come home after a long day of work. They show affection impulsively, but like Taurus, they are always there for you, regardless of their Aries fire.

May 19 - May 20
Taurus with Gemini tendencies. These cats are very persuasive. You may not have wanted to play with the laser toy initially, but the adorable chirps and leg-rubs have convinced you to spend the next half hour whizzing the little red dot around the living room.

GEMINI
May 21st - June 20th

DUALITY: Masculine

ELEMENT: Air

QUALITY: Mutable

PERFECT COLLAR COLOR: Yellow

FAVORITE TOY: Depends on the day

WEAKNESS: Curiosity

The symbol of Gemini is the Twins. So, you may wonder if you accidentally rescued two cats from the local shelter, not one! And like twins often are, each side is the polar opposite of the other. One minute she is sweet and friendly, the next hissy, then literally a hurricane. Boom... she is asleep; out cold.

Serious whiplash! The actions of your cat lead you to believe that if the (admittedly) unlikely "two cats not one" theory is false, then you have perhaps the first clinically diagnosable case of a bipolar cat.

Look on the bright side, at least your cat is never boring to be around!

She is super smart and learns quickly. She is talkative,

constantly jabbering away—she may be talking to you or to herself, it is hard to tell. Everything is a game and a test of her intellect.

Your cat will also play games with you—there is nothing a Gemini cat loves more than a battle of wits. Even better, if you do manage to best her, she is not a sore loser. She respects anyone who can outsmart her. But, do not get too cocky about winning, as it all follows her master plan at the end of the day, and your winning was just step #3,299,873,422 to world domination!

Your cat is curious and her powers of observation will teach her whatever she wants to know. Social and friendly, Gemini cats thrive off of interaction. If you have another cat, rest assured that she is glad for the company as Gemini cats are social butterflies. It stands to reason that with each personality shift, little Miss Scooter bounces from one social interaction to the next, spending a minute headbutting your knees, then scratching the couch, then deleting half a page of your Master's thesis, then antagonizing the dog.

Try not to feel hurt when your cat quickly loses interest in things that used to fascinate her, for example, a favorite toy, comfiest perch... or her owner—she just moves too fast for your human brain. Her motivation is to avoid boredom at all costs, so she has a need to move on and keep things fresh. She will eventually turn her attention back to you when it suits her. She does value your companionship, despite all outward appearances.

You make her happiest by providing a diverse range of entertainment, as she quickly tires of the same old games. Try getting toys with various textures. For wand toys, get interchangeable attachments, and to satisfy her curiosity, always let her smell whatever you have got cooking!

In summary, (if it is possible to summarize a Gemini): A Gemini cat will test your humility—because she has none.
She will test your patience—because she has none.
She will test your love—but she has some.
She has ninety-nine personalities, but tame is not one!

Cusps of Gemini

May 21 - May 25
Gemini with Taurus tendencies. Your cat is curious and inquisitive; and very stubborn. Once she has decided to lay on your keyboard, well—dang it, she will. She makes a good first impression to visitors, but take her outside her comfort zone and she would rather hide.

June 16 - June 20
Gemini with Cancer tendencies. Your cat is talkative but also cautious. She loves her familiar perches and toys and is easily scared by any quick movements or loud noises. She likes to analyze a situation, so you will often catch her frozen in thought, contemplating how something works, remaining impossibly still.

@youngestoldcatlady

When cat fostering advocate Ashley, also known as @youngestoldcatlady, was contacted about a group of severely emaciated and sick kittens by a follower on her Instagram, she knew she had to step in. Four tiny kittens arrived two hours later after a mother and daughter drove them to her home, hoping she could save them. They had been found on the side of the road by another friend, who realized the severity of their illnesses after one of their siblings died.

Licorice was the most ill, to the point he was deformed from malnourishment. Even though the vets suggested that Ashley euthanize, she continued round-the-clock care, with syringe feeding, subcutaneous fluids, vitamin supplements and more. Gradually the kittens began to improve. After almost two months, and multiple setbacks, Licorice and his siblings thrived and were big enough to go to their forever homes. Licorice is now happy and healthy in his forever home with his brother Skittles.

CANCER
June 21st - July 22nd

DUALITY: Feminine

ELEMENT: Water

QUALITY: Cardinal

PERFECT COLLAR COLOR: Sea green or metallic silver

FAVORITE TOY: Silver crinkle balls

WEAKNESS: Getting lost in the closet

There is a Cancer cat called Cornelius; he is very sensitive to his surroundings, dislikes strangers, and anything new is scary.

Due to Cornelius's many insecurities and trust issues (he sees a therapist twice a week), he can come across as a real CAT! He is hissy and quick to bat strangers away with his paws if he gets cornered; preferring to dart from the room, pausing for a second to look over his shoulder with wide eyes, before disappearing in the labyrinth of hiding places in the guest bedroom.

Despite his faults, Cornelius is also the best friend

a person could ask for. He can tell when you are having a bad day, and unlike some cats, he cares enough to try and make you feel better. Cornelius will lay against your legs when you are reading on the couch, and patiently sit on the bathroom counter while watching you brush your teeth.

Like the crab that represents Cancer, Cornelius has a tough exterior that hides his inner softness.

Because your Cancer cat is so sensitive to others' emotions and energy, he does much better with people he knows. However, it is a universal truth that all friends were once strangers. Patience is key to slowly introducing your Cancer cat to your friends over weeks or months. As he learns to trust that your friend is not going to hurt his sensitive heart, he will come out of his shell. Try to keep these visits stable, for instance, have your friend come over to watch a movie weekly. Having the same activity and energy level for each visit will reassure your Cancer cat that he can know what to expect when your friend comes over.

If you have a Cancer cat like Cornelius at home, respect that STRANGERS = BAD and that is never going to change. If you are going to have a get-together at your house, make sure to have an "off-limits-to-humans" part of the house with lots of hiding places (and a litter box) all within reach so that your Cancer cat does not feel like there is no escape.

Cancer cats are ruled by the Moon, so as the Moon changes throughout the month, watch for changes in your cat as well. The tricky thing about astrology is that it affects everyone; you and your cat are subject to the same energy pulls, both in terms of sensitivity and emotion. Unchecked, this can lead you and your cat to be frustrated with each other. Cancer cats especially can let emotion and intuition overrule logic and reason, so they are strongly controlled by the astrology of the day. However, as the human, you can be conscious of that energy and change your behavior to best serve your cat.

Cusps of Cancer

June 21 - June 25
Cancer with Gemini tendencies. Your cat needs change and excitement to keep his Gemini side happy, however moving too quickly can jar confidence. Always make one change at a time in order to keep things fresh but safe, for example, if you need to change the type of litter box and the location of the litter box, allow time for your cat to get used to the new box in the old location before beginning to move the box to the new location.

July 18 - July 22
Cancer with Leo tendencies. Your cat accepts new people into the house without much fuss, however it takes him a while to acknowledge their presence, much less be visibly excited to see them. After all, he is much more focused on how stately visitors must think he looks walking down the hall, showing his rear.

@puppykittynycity

It was late October in New York City when a passerby noticed that the box on top of the trash bins was not empty. Inside was little Snowflake; she was three months old and abandoned. Lucky for her, Puppy Kitty NYC got the call and whisked her out of the cold and into a foster home, where she was fully vetted and soon found her forever home. PKNYC helps kittens just like Snowflake, but also extreme medical cases like Marshall who was found with a severed leg needing extensive medical attention, and feral cats needing to be Trapped, Neutered and Returned (TNR'd). TNR is the most humane way to control overpopulation for neighborhood cats who would not be able to transition to indoor life. This way, feral cats can live out their natural lives in the only way they ever knew—except without producing more kittens.

"The difference between cats and genius is that genius has limits"

- Some Science Cat

LEO
July 23rd - August 22nd

DUALITY: Masculine

ELEMENT: Fire

QUALITY: Fixed

PERFECT COLLAR COLOR: Gold and orange

FAVORITE TOY: The tallest cat tree so as to survey the kingdom

WEAKNESS: None, obviously.

Fade in:

Exterior of a suburban home in daytime

Neatly cut lawn, beige siding and a single tree

Camera zooms through tree branches and window:

Interior of home

Enter HONEY with a flourish. With almost comical theatricality, she waltzes across the set with her tail held high, exuding the energy and confidence of a queen—which she is. Nose in the air, she hops onto

*the opposite end of the couch as her owner, circles
once, then lays down.*

Human:
"So, when exactly were you going to tell me that
we were in a movie about your life?

Honey:
"It started when I was born. I assumed that you
were aware."

Human:
"I knew that you were born to be famous. I know
that you think you are the greatest cat that ever
lived, God's gift to humankind, the Queen of the
house..."

Honey:
"You basically can't wait to get home and hang
out with me because, and I quote, 'Oh Em Gee,
she is soooo funny!'"

Human:
"And you know it. But that comes at a price. Others
do not like people who are so full of themselves."

Honey:
"I am not people. I am a cat."

Human:
"Let's do Pros/Cons. Like your horoscope sign, Leo,
the Lion, you are brave, loyal and protective."

Honey:

"And awesome. Do not forget awesome. And every other positive word in the limited human dictionary."

Human:
"Awesome. Fine. Cons: you can be jealous and over dramatic. I am not allowed to ignore you or leave you alone for more than a work day. As soon as I get home, I have to pay my respects, say hello to you, tell you how pretty you are and ask about your day. You never ask me back! And what do I get in return? You scratch my couch."

Silence in the living room. The human shifts uncomfortably. Honey gets to her feet and stretches, slowly extending her back legs and arching her back. She yawns and pads over to her owner and flops onto his lap. She purrs contentedly.

Honey:
"I love when we talk about me."

Fade out.

As you can tell by the screenplay, Leo cats are pretty self-centered. However, you can cater to their ego in order to create a peaceful home environment. A Leo cat who believes that she is your number one priority is a happy cat. Ironically, for a Leo cat to feel like the center of attention, she needs you. She does love you! Her identity depends on receiving your attention and affection. She will put up with your absence, but is always glad to see you when you return.

Because of their overwhelming joy at your return,

in this moment Leo cats may scratch things even more than other cats. The good news is that a cat scratcher is more appealing than a couch, however it is all about location. If the scratcher is not near the entryway where your cat feels the compulsion to express their joy at your return, they will go for whatever option is closest. Make sure to have a good scratching option (vertical or horizontal, depending on your cat's preference) near where your cat typically scratches.

Or just get used to the fact that your couch is ruined because your little Leo is the ruler of your kingdom. Bow down.

Cusps of Leo

July 23 - July 27
Leo with Cancer tendencies. These cats love a good brain teaser; give them a puzzle toy and they will work it until it is done, thanks to their ability to concentrate. They can be a little possessive about their relationships—once they lay on your lap, you must stay put.

August 18 - August 22
Leo with Virgo tendencies. Determination is strong in these cats. If there is a ledge just out of reach, rest assured (or lay awake at night knowing) your cat will find a way to get up there. These cats also make choices instinctually, and ask questions later, giving you more reason to worry about them... All. The. Time.

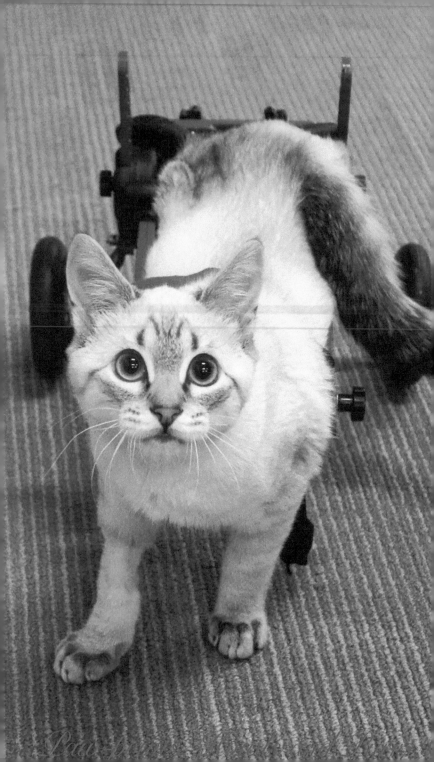

Paw-prints, Howls and Purrs!©

@mojoshope

Just so you know, HarPURR's mom is a superstar; she kept HarPURR alive outdoors even though he only had use of his front legs. At three weeks old, he was found by Tundra Cat Rehabilitation and then found a foster through Mojo's Hope, the partner organization to @alaskaskaaats. He needed socialization, but since he had not finished his vaccinations yet, he found a friend in Cinder, his foster parents' gentle dog. The two love cuddling and taking naps together. Once he was big enough, HarPURR was fitted for a little wheelchair and now he loves to chase toys on his new wheels!

Mojo's Hope is a small all-volunteer 501(c)(3) non-profit rescue group for animals with special needs based in Anchorage, Alaska.

VIRGO
August 23rd - September 22nd

DUALITY: Feminine

ELEMENT: Earth

QUALITY: Mutable

PERFECT COLLAR COLOR: Dark blue
and gray

FAVORITE TOY: Food puzzle

WEAKNESS: Knocking all the mail off
the table (That's not where it belongs!)

Your Virgo cat strives to be of use. He is a doer and a thinker, and is motivated by his mission. That motivational PURRRpose is of the highest importance, and though he loves you, his life revolves around the all-consuming mission.

We probably do not have a clue as to what that mission may be, but your Virgo cat is clearly invested.

You can tell when he darts from one end of the house to the other for seemingly no reason at all, he is doing it in service to the Mission. Some Virgo cats choose the Mission of ridding the world of insects;

others, the Mission of watching every movement from the cat tree by the front window.

Your Virgo cat hates clutter because of his love of precision and neatness. Everything must have a place. Has he peed on a pile of clothes you left because you would "pick them up later"? Uh huh. That was your fault. Keep things orderly and in their place and you will find that your Virgo cat will never have to resort to such measures to get his point across.

Virgo cats are highly analytical; he knows your normal schedule like the back of his paws. Because of his need to analyze and understand a situation, he may get trapped in analysis-paralysis if something new throws a wrench in his carefully laid plans. For example, you bought a new rug for the hallway. He stares at it for hours, unable to cross it to get to his afternoon nap spot. What is he supposed to do? Just walk over it? That was not in his daily schedule before! Everything has changed.

That daily schedule is everything to your cat. He keeps the same schedule every day, waking, eating and sleeping like clockwork.

He is pretty shy and reserved, so make sure he has space to retreat to when strangers come over to the house. However, Virgo cats are people-pleasers, and get immense satisfaction from making their humans happy. He is communicative and loquacious, thanks to his ruling planet Mercury, whom he shares with Gemini cats.

Make sure that any changes to a Virgo's environment are made slowly, a little bit at a time. For example, move the litter box a couple feet at a time in order not to overwhelm your order-loving Virgo cat. Move cat trees the same way. Bring in new furniture before taking out old furniture so your cat can make sense of the new stuff while still holding onto the solid past. Since your cat is so schedule obsessed, keeping a stable schedule for yourself and your cat can go a long way towards keeping him happy.

Other than his freakish need for cleanliness and order, Virgo cats are pretty laid-back. They get along with other pets because they feel no need to be the alpha. Keep things neat and same, same, same, and your Virgo cat will be a steady, loving companion.

Cusps of Virgo

August 23 - August 27
Virgo with Leo tendencies. Sweet, fun and warm, these cats make wonderful companions. He loves to show off his skills because he loves to receive your encouragement.

September 18 - September 22
Virgo with Libra tendencies. Your cat seeks your approval, however it is easy to give it when he is so gregarious and fun to be around. He is a talker and a lover. He likes the best things in life, and loves a clean room. What you do not know is that he is meowing about quantum entanglement.

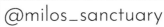

@milos_sanctuary

Milo's Sanctuary & Special Needs Cat Rescue, Inc. is a non-profit 501(c)(3) founded on the belief that all cats deserve a second chance at life, especially those that have physical disabilities, are seniors, have a terminal illness, or have been abused and need someone to care for, love, and understand them.

One of the lifetime residents at Milo's Sanctuary is Sally Fuzzytoes. Blinded by the abuse she experienced on the streets of Cairo, Egypt, Sally came to the sanctuary with severe trust issues. Her only solace was running for hours on a kitty running wheel. The miles made a difference because Sally is now happily meowing for food in the kitchen at Milo's Sanctuary! You can become a Lifetime Care Sponsor for Sally at milossanctuary.org

"Courage is being scared to death but petting the tummy floof anyway"

- Some Old West Cat

LIBRA

September 23rd - October 22nd

DUALITY: Masculine

ELEMENT: Air

QUALITY: Cardinal

PERFECT COLLAR COLOR: Lavender

FAVORITE TOY: An expensive modern
cat tree

WEAKNESS: Sucker for compliments

Why invest in decor for your home when your beautiful Libra cat lives in it? Every move she makes is poetry in motion; a priceless work of art. However, she loves an elegantly curated home, so if you have not already, lay down the big bucks for a luxury cat tree or three.

Your Libran cat is not just a pretty face. She is charming and easy to be around—she makes you feel better with a purr and a blink—she has charisma by the truckload, her personality is magnetic. When people come over, they have trouble focusing on human conversations because her presence is so captivating.

Perhaps the best thing about your Libran cat is that her charisma comes from a good place. She genuinely cares about people. Her partnership with a human or place in a family is so important to her. When you are struggling, she lends a sympathetic ear and listens with understanding and compassion. Though she does not understand the dynamic between you and Sharon at work, your cat will always be there to commiserate.

Since your cat is motivated by her relationships with others, human and otherwise, she does best when you are home. If you are away from home a lot, she might appreciate having another animal for friendship if she does not have a buddy already.

Libran cats avoid confrontation at all costs, so you will often see her lope away instead of engage when another cat pounces on her.

Libran cats sound amazing right? However, like every cat, they do have their weaknesses. They can be entitled, thinking that you should spend all of your money on their every comfort. They can also overindulge on food. Combine that with a preference for naps and laziness over exercise, and a Libran cat could be gaining too much weight. Because your cat wants to please everyone, she may sometimes freeze when there are too many options to consider—try to make what you want from her obvious.

You should keep an eye on your cat's consumption because with weight gain comes all sorts of health issues, for example arthritis. If you free-feed kibble, make sure to track how much you are giving your cat and not just refill the bowl whenever it becomes empty.

For any cat, not just Libran cats, consider feeding wet food as well as or instead of dry, as it helps your cat stay hydrated and maintain urinary and kidney health. If your cat ever struggles to urinate or can only pee a little bit at a time, see a veterinarian immediately as that could be a sign of an urinary tract obstruction. Obstructions are fairly common and, if untreated, lethal.

Cusps of Libra

September 23 - September 27
Libran with Virgo tendencies. These cats love people. They are well-liked, and adore the spotlight. However, they can swing from emotional high to emotional low at the drop of a stale catnip toy.

October 18 - October 22
Libra with Scorpio tendencies. Charismatic and charming, these cats know exactly how to manipulate you to get what they want. You know they are doing it, but who cares? They are so darn cute, you would do anything for them, so what is the harm in letting your cat play with your favorite necklace, anyway?

@wolf_the_catventurer

Walking a cat requires patience! It has taken many days of training for Wolf to become the hiking queen that she is today. Every day, her human would take her outside for the same short walk around the block. As each day passed, Wolf became more and more confident on a leash and harness. She had been found outside, freezing and hungry when she was six or eight weeks old, so getting outside was a return to a former life, of sorts. Her human made sure that Wolf got lots of cuddles and felt safe, even when large trucks or dogs would pass by. She was never forced to walk and so she grew to love being on leash. On her walks, she loves to smell the plants, stare at birds and especially make new friends!

"The cat tree is calling and I must go"

- Some Adventurous Cat

SCORPIO
October 23rd - November 21st

DUALITY: Feminine

ELEMENT: Water

QUALITY: Fixed

PERFECT COLLAR COLOR: What collar?

FAVORITE TOY: Circle racetrack scratcher—the one with the ball that rolls

WEAKNESS: Compulsively shares unsolicited opinions

Scorpio cats are known for their intense loyalty, intense competitiveness and general intensity. They are mysterious, magnetic and graceful.

Loyal to a fault, they are protective of their people and nonhuman friends, but that can cross over into possessiveness. The author's Scorpio cat, River, is a great illustration how this can go down. She is always trying to take care of the author's other cat, Trickle, an independent Aries. She frequently grooms Trickle, who thus far has never reciprocated the grooming urges. All the attention seems to annoy Trickle, who wishes River would just stop tickling her. When Trickle tries to walk away, River rather roughly pins her down and continues grooming her until she is satisfied with her appearance.

Scorpio cats just want control. Give your cat ways to feel in control of her life and you will see the better side of her: loving, loyal, generous and gentle. When the author's dog goes out for his nighttime walk, River paces, clearly upset. She watches out each window, straining to see where he is, meowing pitifully. When he returns she is ecstatic, rubbing on his legs, sniffing him, making sure that no harm befell him while he was outside her protection. In return, he will play bow and pick her up by her scruff; she happily goes limp. It is a strange relationship.

When they are happy, things are 'glowy' and wonderful. However, the storm clouds are always on the horizon for a Scorpio cat.

You do not want to mess with a Scorpio. They have got opinions and can be vengeful if they feel wronged. River is proof of this. When she was forced to wear a cone after her spay surgery, she lasted less than twenty-four hours before she snapped.

The couple had just gotten ready for bed, the lights turned off and lain down when River walked right onto the author's fiancé and peed.

You read that right. She peed on his bare chest!

MESSAGE RECEIVED.

The cone was taken off and her human family has lived in fear of ever crossing her again. Luckily, the wedding is still on.

It is funny now, but the point of retelling the story is not just to illustrate what an angry Scorpio cat is capable of, but also to show how you can work through most things with your cat if you only listen to what they are saying.

It may take some experimentation to figure out what exactly is bothering your cat, especially if the cause is not something so obvious as the 'Cone of Shame'. However fixing the underlying issue will fix whatever your cat is doing to show you that something has upset them.

Cusps of Scorpio

October 23 - October 27
Scorpio with Libran tendencies. These cats can be very stubborn, but only if you ask for something out of the ordinary. The rest of the time, they are friendly and pleasant companions, but they are not clingy.

November 17 - November 21
Scorpio with Sagittarian tendencies. Opinionated and vocal, these cats are always making a scene. Visitors think your cat is judgmental of them, and you tend to agree. Your cat has lots of nervous energy. However, your cat is a loyal squad member and a true ride or die.

@thepowerofozzy

With his blue eyes, striking stripes and fox-like tail, Ozzy could easily be mistaken for cat royalty. He did not come from a long line of designer cats, however... He is a rescue! Ozzy has not known a day without love, food and snuggles since he, his siblings and mother were fostered by @myfosterkittens soon after his birth. Ozzy was so young he still had his umbilical cord attached! They were known as the Napa Valley Kitties and each had a wine themed name. Ozzy was called Foley, and there was Petite Sirah, Helena, Bremer, Jessup and Mama Merlot. You can watch the siblings grow in their forever homes by searching for #napavalleykitties

"Cats are the
teachers of all
things"

- Some Roman Cat

SAGITTARIUS
November 22nd - December 21st

DUALITY: Masculine

ELEMENT: Fire

QUALITY: Mutable

PERFECT COLLAR COLOR: Purple

FAVORITE TOY: Variety packs of springs and little balls of fluff

WEAKNESS: Exploration

Did you once put out food for a visiting cat and they still have not left... years later?

That cat who showed up at your doorstep all that time ago, and that you fed and cared for ever since, is likely Sagittarius.

Sagittarian cats are optimistic, carefree and lucky—they are freedom seekers and wanderers. That cat had struck out for new horizons with the fearlessness an unbroken streak of luck gives a cat and he ended up on your doorstep. See? Lucky.

"No strings attached" is the motto of Sagittarian cats. Though you have fallen in love with Mr Biggles and have pledged your life and discretionary cash to him, he has pledged no such unbreakable vows. He likes you, sure, but he likes pretty much everyone. If you are okay with being just one of the stars in his sky, Mr. Biggles will be your Sun.

Despite having the luckiest lucky streak of all, Sagittarian cats still only have nine lives. We recommend keeping cats indoors to increase their life expectancy, especially if there are wild predators, cars or cold in your area.

The great news is that you do not have to completely force your cat out of the outdoor life. Your cat may love being an "Adventure Cat". "Adventure Cats" are those cats on leashes who go hiking and have millions of followers on Instagram? Travel, adventure and riding on the tops of backpacks are things that are usually hard to convince most cats to enjoy, but if you approach each step slowly and gently, your Sagittarian cat could have potential.

Sagittarius is ruled by Jupiter, the great, big, huggable, confident bundle of fun in the solar system. Sagittarian cats can exude a lot of the swagger that Jupiter lends this sign; they love pretty much everything, but they will often switch between all their interests on a whim, so if yesterday's toy is not cutting it, try something else.

These cats are playful, cute and comical and get

along well with other animals, most of the time. Sagittarian cats do great in large families and busy households because although their love of freedom prevents them from being super attached to just one person, they make friends easily and are always happy to cozy up to just about anyone.

Cusps of Sagittarius

November 22 - November 26
Sagittarius with Scorpio tendencies. Slightly psychic with a dash of psycho. These cats are masters at getting all eyes on them. They are super smart and always ten steps ahead of you. All that said, they love you passionately.

December 17 - December 21
Sagittarius with Capricorn tendencies. Look into his eyes and you see great wisdom. Your cat is friendly and has good manners most of the time. He is very thorough when sweeping the house for shadows, insects and little bits of fluff. He knows exactly who he is, and will not change for anyone. He loves you deeply and holds a special place in his heart for anyone who played a big role in his life, even if it has been years since he saw them.

@wobblycats

This is Sampson. He is a normal cat, just a little wobbly!

Cerebellar Hyperplasia (CH) is a condition where the cerebellum has not fully developed. Since this part of the brain controls voluntary movement, cats with CH are adorably wobbly.

The instagram account @wobblycats shows just how wonderful wobbly life can be with three CH cats, Sampson, Trooper and Frankie. Thank you to the CatNap Society, Victoria Humane Society and Bradshaw Animal Shelter for having these beautiful kitties up for adoption because they make thousands of people happy.

"We have two lives,
and the second
begins when you
meet your cat"

- Some Philosopher Cat

CAPRICORN
December 22nd - January 19th

DUALITY: Feminine

ELEMENT: Earth

QUALITY: Cardinal

PERFECT COLLAR COLOR: Mossy
green or brown

FAVORITE TOY: A scratching post that
she can perch on top of

WEAKNESS: Sometimes a tripping
hazard

Muffins always knows best and you should do things HER way.

Capricorn cats are serious, steady, patient and determined. They are often found patiently stalking a leaf with intense concentration, sometimes waiting for many minutes to pass before striking.

Despite all of her seriousness and gravity, Muffins has a surprising sense of humor that can come out when you least expect it. That long-awaited pounce on the leaf may become a mad hopping dash through the house, her tail held crooked like she just saw a cucumber.

Capricorn cats believe that they know best. Even though she has never fried an egg in her life, Muffins will still want to supervise every step of the process to make sure you are doing it right.

Instead of pushing her away and trying to stop her meddling, set up some boundaries that allow her to supervise, but still be out of your way. Just because she has the traits of a good leader, does not mean she is a good manager.

Do this by setting up a safe perch to supervise from, away from open flames.

Because Capricorn cats are self-sufficient and sometimes described as cold, they can have trouble in their relationships with other cats. If your domestic bliss is interrupted by scuffles between the feline forces of the house, there are some things you can try.

Cats do not figure things out by, for example, establishing dominance in a fight. Make sure to break up fights by clapping your hands or spraying them with your houseplant mister. As each cat is the Center of the Universe (apparently quantum mechanics will eventually explain this), there cannot be one Center of the Universe in dominance over another. Keep up. Put more simply, cats evolved to be loners, so their conflict resolution skills are weak.

Make sure to have a litter box, food bowl, water bowl and perches for each cat throughout the house so none of these items can be guarded. For example, have one food bowl in the laundry room and the other in the spare room, so one cat cannot hover over both bowls, therefore preventing your other cat from eating.

Try feel-good pheromones. What?! Cats release pheromones through their paws and face that leave messages for other cats, but also for themselves. Here is an example. *Rub: I like this thing. Next time I smell this, I will remember.* Synthetic pheromone dispensers can really help by circulating the happy vibes specifically formulated for easing interaction for multiple cats in a household.

For more tips on how to get your cats to live in peace, check out ASPCA in the United States, RSPCA in the United Kingdom, or International Cat Care Charity.

It is important to note that any abrupt change in cat behavior is worth a trip to the veterinarian to rule out underlying health issues.

Cusps of Capricorn

December 22 - December 26
Capricorn with Sagittarian tendencies. You can never really tell what your cat is thinking. Beneath that deadpan stare is a heart that cares when you hurt, and celebrates when you are happy. A

potential flight risk, make sure to watch the door when you are bringing in the groceries.

January 15 - January 19
Capricorn with Aquarius tendencies. Generous, your cat is a lover of people and community. She is loyal and fierce when wronged. Her social nature hides the deep thinker inside.

Eddy Spaghetti...

Eddy Spaghetti was a feral cat for four years before he was caught for trap-neuter-return, but he was deemed to have the right temperament to become an indoor kitty! Despite his good looks and very unique nose/fur color combination, he spent some time in foster care, as the status of being a FIV+ cat seemed to scare away potential adopters.

@eddy_spaghetti_cat

and The Meatballs!

Tilty G. and her brother **Rambo** (~2 years old) were rescued by the Humane Society, but little is known about their life prior to being saved. Like Eddy, they are FIV+, but they also have other qualities that make them extra special! Just like her name implies, Tilty has a permanent head tilt, but this does not seem to impact her quality of life whatsoever! As for Rambo, he became the one-eyed wonder shortly after being rescued, as they needed to remove his infected eye.

Be positive! FIV+ cats are!

Feline Immunodeficiency Virus slowly affects a cat's immune system over years. But what does that mean? It means years of high quality life and a normal lifespan for most cats affected.

Yes, these cats need yearly veterinary exams and any symptoms of sickness should immediately be checked out by a vet, but that is what all cat owners should do regardless of their cat's positivity.

FIV is not easily transferred from cat to cat, since it requires a deep bite wound. Keeping FIV+ cats indoors and in peaceful coexistence with other cats prevents the spread of this disease. Many people adopt only FIV+ cats so they can all live positively ever after.

"Let thy cat be thy medicine"

- Some Cat Long Ago

AQUARIUS
January 20th - February 18th

DUALITY: Masculine

ELEMENT: Air

QUALITY: Fixed

PERFECT COLLAR COLOR: Sky blue

FAVORITE TOY: Empty toilet paper roll

WEAKNESS: Cannot stay still

Aquarius is ruled by the planet Uranus... which says a lot about Aquarians.

Uranus does not even know how to be a proper planet—it spins on its side. That oddball influence of Uranus makes Aquarian cats much more likely to forge their own path.

Aquarian cats are different, quirky, and eccentric. For instance, Roxy is easygoing except she has to knock any pens found on the kitchen table to the floor. Just pens. Tom rips paper to shreds. Wilbur rolls on dirty socks. It is clear that store-bought cat toys will lie disused and ignored, wasted on an Aquarian cat that does not appreciate the engineering that goes into a cat toy that "flies like a real bird".

They like to rebel for the sake of being a rebel. They are also extremely obstinate and refuse to back down from a seemingly irrational opinion. It is not that they do not respect your opinion, they just have to push their theory to its limits, because of their scientist-cat nature. Despite a major need to be a unique individual, Aquarian cats are not loners. Aquarius rules the eleventh house of the zodiac of teamwork and friendship, so it is no wonder they are such great companions.

As the Water Bearer, (but not a water sign— Aquarius is an Air sign like Libra and Gemini) Aquarian cats are givers and want you to be happy. They are big on communication and constantly share information through meows, purrs, chirps, and touch.

All that energy can make them restless during the night. In order to give yourself the best chance of a good night's sleep without all their eccentric nighttime activities keeping you up, put them through a replica of the natural cycle of all cats: hunt, eat, clean, sleep.

How can this regime be achieved?

First, take care of everything you need to do before bed; brush your teeth, put on your cat-themed jammies and turn off the TV. Now entertain your cat with a wand toy, giving him a chance to feel like the hunter that he is. If he refuses to play with a store bought toy, tie a string to a capped pen or crumpled piece of paper. After a spirited fight, he will finally "kill" the prey. Then, serve your cat his food. Get into bed as soon as possible while your cat finishes his food and then starts to compulsively groom himself.

Should he start tickling your face with his whiskers as you sleep several hours later, give him a big hug and tell him that he cannot leave the bed until morning. His horror and natural need to be free and revolt against restraint will make him disappear until morning!

Cusps of Aquarius

January 20 - January 24
Aquarius with Capricorn tendencies. Your cat is his own man. Independent, he vacillates between social piranha and social pariah. He has a great memory and has a first-rate mental catalog of all the smells he has ever smelt on your shoes.

February 14 - February 18
Aquarius with Pisces tendencies. Your cat cannot be rushed, wanting to fully examine every new situation before proceeding. Despite that seriousness, he is quite carefree. He gets along with most people, perhaps because of the Pisces influence that heightens intuition and ability to sense spirits, lending him a deeper sense of empathy with others.

When her owner could not keep her, TLC was brought to Santa Barbara Humane Society. She was having skin irritation and was heavily overweight. The extra weight was not helping her mobility, since she had a birth defect that made one of her back legs almost useless. Staff lovingly called her "Kickstand" from the way she would stand with her leg stretched out to the side. Basically, TLC needed some serious TLC. The medical team at SB Humane put her on a diet and cleared up her skin irritation. At the time of writing, TLC has lost three pounds, her skin has cleared up with the help of medication and she is up for adoption! TLC also enjoys training new cat volunteers because she loves all people and craves attention.

PISCES
February 19th - March 20th

DUALITY: Feminine

ELEMENT: Water

QUALITY: Mutable

PERFECT COLLAR COLOR: Turquoise

FAVORITE TOY: The sink

WEAKNESS: Easily frightened

The circle of life—the signs of the zodiac are meant to be a circle. Every year has a beginning and end, and so does the zodiac. Pisces is the last sign of the zodiac, so where Aries signified fire, initiation, and beginnings, Pisces signifies eternity and reincarnation. If you have ever sworn that you found your childhood cat decades later... that is a totally Pisces cat thing to do.

You may be saying, "that is a little woo woo", but wait there is more! Pisces cats are extra spiritual. Yes, cats can be spiritual; they have been worshipped many times over the past ten thousand years, so it would be weird if they were not spiritual.

Being so spiritual, Pisces cats can see ghosts. All cats can see ghosts, but Pisces cats are particularly obsessed with watching them, meowing at them, and taking swipes at them. Have you ever seen your cat staring into space, mouth open, eyes wide? Ever watched your cat leap up the wall to catch what exactly, you never know? Does she ever stare over your shoulder at nothing? The answer is ghosts. There is not really any advice for that, but at least you now know why she has been doing this all these years.

Pisces cats are intuitive, perceptive and sympathetic, so they make great therapy cats. They are especially successful with people with developmental disabilities because they step into the role of comforter and teacher with grace and compassion.

Since your cat will not stand up for herself, you may have to assume the role of protector. As a cat parent, it is your responsibility to speak for her. Regardless of how patient and conflict-averse your cat is, she still needs protection and firm personal boundaries.

All that sensitivity and empathy means Pisces cats are a great judge of character. They are sensitive to the energy of the people around them. If they do not like someone, take heed. They may be sensing bad intentions, but their reaction to a person may not be for as dark a reason as that. They may simply sense this person is wrong for you at this moment, or that a difference of opinion could cause conflict at this time in your life. People are always changing and evolving, so just because your cat got bad vibes from someone one time, does not mean that they always will. When your Pisces cat speaks up about a person, use that as a reminder to heighten your own senses around that individual.

Pisces cats are giving and selfless—but they are still cats! Even though they have been worshipped over the years, they are still flawed. Pisces cats deal with inner conflict a lot. The symbol of two fishes swimming in different directions shows the conflict that wanting to give everything but also being a cat, can cause. This internal conflict can make Pisces cats seem scattered and frantic—sitting on a lap to give comfort, then hiding from the spirits in the bookcase, eyes wide with terror.

Cusps of Pisces

February 19 - February 23
Pisces with Aquarius tendencies. Your cat enjoys new toys and climbers; she is elegant with refined tastes in food; she becomes very determined when she sets a goal. And, she will continue leaping up the wall until she finally catches the scuff mark.

March 16 - March 20
Pisces with Aries tendencies. Your cat has an outgoing personality that makes her many friends. She loves to tease—you will find she asks for pets, then walks away as soon as you kneel at her level. Original and eclectic with her tastes, she will always surprise you.

Author's Conclusion

If we do not laugh, we will cry.

And honestly, I have never seen people laugh more than when I explain that I have written a book about astrology for cats.

The idea is to make you laugh.

More importantly, it is also about saving lives.

Due to my personal experience in animal welfare, I have seen firsthand how cats can be relinquished due to issues that could have been fixed if the person had only known what to try. However, by the time they walk into the shelter, they are at their wit's end and they have already made the decision to give up.

Now, I know perhaps two people who read about cat behavior and psychology, but most good cat behavior books strangely do not go viral.

I hope Feline Astrology is the book that will end up in the hands of cat owners before they come to breaking point. Maybe it was a gift from a friend who knew they loved cats, or they picked it up and flipped through it at the cat cafe.

But, it was there when their cat started peeing

outside the litter box. The information was in their mind when they were having people over for Cinco de Mayo and they just adopted a timid Pisces.

The reader now knows what the Trap–Neuter–Return (TNR) program is, that feline immunodeficiency virus (FIV) is not a death sentence, and that cats with Cerebellar Hyperplasia can still have full, happy lives.

So, if feline astrology lessons get these life-saving messages into more hands... well, that is really something to laugh about, and celebrate.

Nonprofit Information

Alaskas KAAATS
501(c)3
www.facebook.com/AlaskasKaaats

Milo's Sanctuary, Inc.
501(c)3
www.milossanctuary.org/

Mojo's Hope
501(c)3
www.mojoshope.org/donate/

Little Wanderers
501(c)3
www.littlewanderersnyc.org/

Puppy Kitty NYCity (PKNYC)
501(c)3
https://puppykittynyc.org/

Santa Barbara Humane Society
501(c)3
www.sbhumanesociety.org

Original Quotes

VI Coco Chanel: "Beauty begins the moment you decide to be yourself."

6 Mahatma Gandhi: "Be the change you want to see in the world."

14 William Shakespeare: "When words fail, music speaks."

25 Albert Einstein: "The difference between stupidity and genius is that genius has limits."

36 John Wayne: "Courage is being scared to death but saddling up anyway."

42 John Muir: "The mountains are calling and I must go."

48 Julius Caesar: "Experience is the teacher of all things."

53 Confucius: "We have two lives and the second begins when we realize we only have one."

60 Hippocrates: "Let thy food be thy medicine."

Acknowledgments

First off, this book would not be what it is without the contributions of all the Instagram accounts featured throughout the pages. I initially thought that reaching out to use other people's pictures and share their stories would be awkward and annoying. It was with trepidation, but with the knowledge that this was going to serve a higher purpose and was therefore necessary (wow, I feel like a movie villain saying that), that I sent out those first few DM's. I was astounded and humbled by the universal willingness of fellow cat lovers to share their stories. I hope you, the reader, were inspired by the stories of special needs and rescue cats.

Thank you Charlita of @wobblycats, Meagan of Puppy Kitty NYC, Michele of Milo's Sanctuary, Shannon of Mojo's Hope and Alaskaskaaats, Lisa of Little Wanderers, Courtney of @eddy_spaghetti_cat, everyone at Santa Barbara Humane Society (you know who you are), Ashley of @youngestoldcatlady, Robin of @thepowerofozzy, Karine of @wolf_the_catventurer and Deanna of @sister.tippy.cat.

Thank you to all the animal rescue workers, veterinary staff, fosters and volunteers in the world who make saving lives possible. You deserve more recognition and support.

Thank you to my editor Rachel Bell for helping me be a better writer, my parents for always being so supportive, and Tim for still loving me even though I spent all my free time on this book and River peed on him once.

Lastly, thank you to the hundreds of cats that I have had the honor to meet over the years, who have taught me so much more than a book ever could.

About the Author

Clair Lofthouse obviously likes cats but she was raised by wolves—well, herding dogs. Nevertheless, she found out that she is a cat person when she began working at a local animal shelter. She is the faithful servant of Jessie (a Catahoula Leopard dog and Rat Terrier cross), River (a Domestic Shorthair Cat) and Trickle (a Cat and Unicorn cross). This is her first book.

CPSIA information can be obtained
at www.ICGtesting.com
Printed in the USA
BVHW022337070619
550509BV00001B/1/P